Forgiveness

The Antidote

Jeri Darby

First Printing 2019
Printed in the United States of America

ISBN: 978-1-958811-04-7

Contact Information:
Jeri Darby 989 402-4721

jeri@iamawriternow.com
Facebook: Jeri Darby

Join my email list:	**Visit my online Bookstore:**

FOR
WE WRESTLE
NOT AGAINST FLESH AND BLOOD,
BUT AGAINST PRINCIPALITIES,
AGAINST POWERS,
AGAINST THE RULERS OF THE
DARKNESS OF THIS WORLD,
AGAINST SPIRITUAL WICKEDNESS
IN HIGH PLACES.

EPHESIANS 6:12 KJV

Table of Contents

Foreword

I have done a forgiveness series on periscope and in a blog. I felt led to repeat this series during a weekly (Monday) Facebook live vlog titled "Seasoned for this Season." I planned to do a single session, but the Holy Spirit prompted me to continue this topic for the following two weeks.

Along with this came an inner prompting to complete this book, which I started and placed on my list over ten years ago. I have a list of subjects and titles I plan to release at the set time. But this one propelled its way to the birthing position of my spiritual womb. This was followed by my sister and dear friend, Minister Patricia Hampton, asking me to host a forgiveness conference in the next eight weeks where I could offer my books. "Great! I will also have my book on this topic ready."

At first—this seemed like a worthy challenge, a conference with my completed book; why not add a workbook? Oh yeah, some real-life dramatizations would be nice. I got this! During the seed stage, it all seemed doable. Then I began feeling seriously overwhelmed! After all, I am a writing coach with clients, writing my own books, all while working full time.

You guessed it…I panicked at what seemed an impossible feat. I was tempted to cancel this commitment, though I felt like this was what God wanted me to accomplish. Then I thought, how can I say that God asked me to fast-track a book and then tell Him I can't do it? We really can do all things through Christ.

This book is a quick read on purpose. Its intent is for the reader to grasp the information and utilize the techniques offered to win the battle with unforgiveness. God desires to answer our prayers, prosper, and heal us. Too many are stuck in revolving cycles of unforgiveness. God can and will liberate you. Align yourself with the directions in His word to be healed and discipline your life to choose forgiveness—*always.*

DEDICATION

THIS BOOK IS DEDICATED TO MY HEAVENLY FATHER
WHO CALLED ME OUT OF DARKNESS AND ACCEPTED ME INTO
HIS BELOVED FAMILY. THANK YOU FOR PRONOUNCING THESE
LIFE-GIVING WORDS OVER MY LIFE:
*"YOU ARE THE KING'S DAUGHTER AND YOU ARE HERE FOR
OFFICIAL BUSINESS."*
THEY HAVE SERVED AS A COMPASS FOR HOPE AND DIRECTION.

TO HIS WONDERFUL SON, JESUS WHO OFFERED HIMSELF FOR
THE FORGIVENESS OF MY SIN AND HAS BEEN WITH ME
THROUGH EVERY DARK SEASON AND FIERY TRIAL. THANK YOU
FOR ALLOWING ME THE USE OF THE POWER AND AUTHORITY
THAT IS IN YOUR NAME!

TO THE HOLY SPIRIT WHO LEADS, GUIDES, COMFORTS,
STRENGTHENS, COUNSELS AND SO MUCH MORE. THANKS FOR
PATIENTLY PRODDING ME FORWARD DURING THE MUNDANE
AND DISILLUSIONED SEASONS OF MY LIFE. THANK YOU FOR
HELPING ME TO UTILIZE THE ANTIDOTE OF FORGIVENESS TO
RELEASE MYSELF AND OTHERS.

I PLEDGE MY ALLEGIANCE TO YOU ALL!

Introduction

Forgiveness is crucial during these perilous times. Things are seldom as they seem. Drama, negative attitudes, and grudges are glamorized in the music and film industries. These unhealthy practices have infiltrated our culture. Clichés like *"I feel some type of way"* are repeated by many to indicate emotional dis-ease. It is not only the younger generation absorbing these dysfunctional influences, but older adults have stooped to immature levels of self-expression. These days, you can just about tell what docudrama one watches by the way they deal with conflict.

The Bible clearly warns that in these last days, there would be division and animosity in the home amongst family members. Misunderstandings occur, and walls of unforgiveness are erected, resulting in years of disunion. Such disunions often result in permanent damage. Why? Because no one wants to be the **FIRST** to apologize; as if this is a sign of mortal weakness.

Unforgiveness works like a poison infiltrating the victim's spiritual, physical, and emotional being. In fact, many have described unforgiveness this way; *"It is like drinking poison and waiting for the other person to die!"* Ridiculous as it sounds, this scenario is acted out and replayed in too many lives. I have two brothers who both required open-heart surgery—*TWICE!* What did these two have in common? Besides being brothers, they both ingested high doses of unforgiveness over the course of their lives.

Unforgiveness has reached epidemic levels in the spiritual body as well as those who refuse to surrender their lives to God because they are angry at others, the church, or God Himself. There *IS* an antidote for the venom that has infected so many. The remedy for what is ailing the inhabitants of this world is abundant in supply, but it is too often left shelved and unused.

For those with the humility and courage to utilize this potent remedy; it brings a remarkable change. Inner wounds oozing hatred and bitterness began to heal. Stony hearts once again

1

become flesh. Stormy emotions recess into a peaceful calm. There are numerous testimonies of miraculous physical healings following surrendering to the process of forgiveness.

Have you been poisoned with unforgiveness venom? Do you feel it working its way through your system? Have you noticed the destructive impact that it has on your mind, body, spirit, and soul? Are you ready to be healed? If so, there is hope! Forgiveness *IS* the antidote. It's the only effective cure to disarm the toxic path of unforgiveness. The supply is limited only by one's reluctance to surrender. It is free, abundant, and available to all.

I pray that this book will benefit those willing not only to recognize but ACT (A) Acknowledge that you have unforgiveness concerns that need to be resolved. (C) Confront-Face those that you have aught with. (T) Trust the Holy Spirit to guide you through the process.

Once you have taken the antidote (forgiveness), don't compare your response to that of others who have done this. For some, inner healing may occur instantly; for many, it will be a process. Whether your recovery is immediate or over a period of time; this is one cure you don't want to dismiss. You can experience the healing powers of forgiveness today.

Prologue

Ri-nng, Ri-nng, Ri-nng...I prayed while waiting for her to answer. Had I attempted this conversation any earlier, my pain-filled words would have slashed her to pieces! "Hello." Her cheerful greeting filled my ears.

"Hello..." We exchanged a few niceties and I revealed the reason for my call. "I was really hurt by your words..." I shared how my emotions were wounded by her remarks that I received as insensitive and attacking. My heart had been weighed down with pain all week.

Yes, I could have readily responded, but I knew my words would not have been fruitful. I did not trust myself to confront her without consulting and receiving direction from the Holy Spirit. I know the power of words and I try to take care not to release poisoned ones. Though I loved this person, I am not able to move forward in relationships, responding as if nothing ever happened.

She readily recalled the situation and replied, "I knew something was bothering you, but I did not know that was it." I was shocked to hear that she was clueless about the negative impact of her words. Mind you, I am not easily shaken; but when fiery darts are from those close to you, they are even more deadly. She continued with words expressing such love, honor, and humility throughout our conversation.

We exchanged words of forgiveness. As we spoke something unexplainable was occurring in my heart. It was like an open gaping wound in my heart was being miraculously repaired. This was definitely a supernatural work of the Holy Spirit. By the end of our conversation, the pain subsided and all that remained was my heart surging with love and compassion.

When teaching about forgiveness; it goes back and forth as to exactly who forgiveness is for. But let's face it; God so loved the world (meaning everyone). satan can influence people to do inhumane actions to others, but this does not exempt them from

3

the love and forgiveness of God. Are you going to deprive yourself of the healing properties of forgiveness, because it just might have some positive benefits for the other person? I pray that you choose forgiveness and allow God to deal with anyone that has caused you pain.

"Father,
Forgive them for they know
Not what they do."

Luke 23:34

Didn't See *THAT* Coming!

It starts as a simple interaction between a husband and wife. Or perhaps a mother and daughter or maybe a father and son. What about friends or church members? Oh! Let's not omit those co-workers! It doesn't matter—w*herever, whenever, whosoever;* if there are *two* or more people gathered and words exchanged, there exists a potential breeding ground for unforgiveness.

Innocent chit-chat fueled by angry words can suddenly become heated, hostile, and bitter. Defensive walls are erected, and each person can walk away with seeds of unforgiveness sown in the fertile ground of their hearts. satan is quick to further pollute emotions with rage, resentment, and rejection...and like weeds, these seeds produce a deadly harvest. If left unaddressed; the love, respect, and unity these people may have once shared is choked and vaporizes into thin air. They wonder why their attempts to communicate their pain to each other fail, not recognizing that they are engaged in a spiritual battle.

satan eagerly intrudes and serves as an interpreter—as if they are speaking foreign languages. With perceptions tarnished by anger, both parties risk failing to hear what the other person is *trying* to say. Anger can cause ears and hearts to open to the whispered lies of satan. Before the words of the speaker can be heard and clearly decoded by the receiver, satan intervenes, twisting and misinterpreting everything the speaker really meant. The more effort put into resolving the conflict, the more twisted the communication becomes. Hostilities increase either ending the relationship altogether or establishing a new distance. Sound familiar?

Such disruptions occur constantly amongst family, friends and co-workers. Anywhere two or more people are exchanging words for *any* purpose the potential for anger, misunderstandings, and unforgiveness exists. Each person may later question, "Why did I say that? How can I fix this? I really didn't mean it!" Yet no matter how regretful they feel their damaging words released in fury cannot be recalled.

Unforgiveness is a quick-acting venom and the heart is its target organ. It quickly infiltrates the heart, causing it to become stony towards the person or persons who inflicted the wound. Before long, there is no longer remorse or desire to repair the damage, and all that remains is angry emotions.

Forgiveness is a potent antidote that counteracts the afflicting symptoms of unforgiveness. It is given unto us by God to defeat our diabolical enemy who has deceived people into thinking that forgiveness creates rather than relieves pain. Or that the person that they are forgiving is undeserving and will be getting off *TOO* easy. Because this affliction does not receive timely treatment, it festers. The poison that is released has a neutralizing effect on the fruit of the Spirit. Love begins to grow cold. This sudden drop in the temperature of love pumping through the spiritual heart causes it to harden.

If unforgiveness remains unaddressed, defensive walls are erected, and few, if any, are able to penetrate the walls of distrust. This attempt is to protect the heart from further injury at all costs. As you continue to distance yourself from others; satan backs you into a corner where you isolate yourself. In that corner, he continues to act as an interpreter of your interactions with others. Because unforgiveness is such a potent poison and can spread easily from person to person; it targets relationships of any and all kinds.

Our fight is not with flesh and blood! We need to grasp this spiritual reality! The Bible warns in 2 Corinthians 2:11 not to be ignorant of satan's devices, yet people are inflicted and defeated by unforgiveness throughout the world in epidemic proportions. Many have not grasped the reality that unforgiveness is one of satan's most destructive weapons! Study the 6th Chapter of Ephesians and pray for the Holy Spirit to teach you how to adorn yourself with the full armor of God. We do not need to go through life unprotected from satan's destructive attacks. We do not have to experience spiritual or physical death resulting from the impact of unforgiveness in our hearts. Read further to gain strategies to fight the good fight of faith and protect yourself from overdosing on unforgiveness.

Forgiveness

Spiritual Exercise

*F*orgiveness is both a powerful and effective spiritual weapon. The more it is utilized the more skilled we become with mastering it. Once we open our eyes to this reality, we will be ready to embrace new potential to engage in effective spiritual warfare. Unfortunately, forgiving is seen by many as a weakness and its powers of liberation tend to be underestimated and underutilized. Thus, many continue to function at a disadvantage and struggle through life, shouldering the debilitating burden of unforgiveness. When healthy relationship are filled with animosity or emotional ties are completely severed—can these relationships be restored?

There is hope— forgiveness is an antidote. An antidote is a medicine given to counteract a *particular* poison. After taking medicine to recover, it is yet necessary to eat right (God's word) and exercise (building strength and endurance). When a person is disciplined in spiritual practices, forgiveness can also become second nature with repetitions. At first, you may feel awkward and clueless about how to approach bridging the uncomfortable distance created by unforgiveness. With practice, it becomes a normal response to offense without a second thought.

The Bible says, *"For physical exercise is of limited value, but godliness is valuable in every way, holding promise for the present life and for the one to come."* (I Timothy 4:8 NIV) Do you know people who are *extremely* committed to exercising? Those whose top priority is keeping their physical bodies fine-tuned. Not knocking it—I would love to be counted among this group! Well, exercising our spirit is just as important. When we are spiritually fit and mindful to perform routine spiritual exercises such as bible reading, prayer, humility, kindness—and forgiveness, they too become second nature. For the longest when leaving home, I could never remember whether I closed the garage door.

My family did not find this humorous, as I would call and ask them to check. This required someone getting out of bed to check several times a week—*early* morning. The remote for the garage door is right above my head in the sun visor of my car. Sometimes, I left it open, but it began to occur fewer and fewer times until this inclination suddenly vanished! I kept calling for them to check because I could not remember if I had shut it.

One day, my grandson, Joseph, was in the car with me, and we reached to close the garage door at the same time. I apologized for always calling home for him to make sure I had shut it—and it was always closed. He laughed and said, "Grandma! *It is muscle memory!*"

Merriam-Webster's online dictionary defines muscle memory as "the ability to repeat a specific muscular movement with improved efficiency and accuracy that is acquired *through practice and repetition."* Jesus said that forgiveness should be offered seventy times seven if needed during a single day! That sounds repetitious to me!

There are people on this earth who are tortured, enslaved, or living in extremely abusive environments. Nothing short of the supernatural power of God will enable them to forgive. This is *not* the reality for most of us. Too often, people cling to a single offense, refusing to employ the antidote of forgiveness, which is a proven cure.

Forgiveness exercises require stretching beyond emotional comfort, the need to be right, and the false belief that you are doing it *only* for the other person. Unforgiveness is a burden too heavy for anyone to bear. It requires surrendering to Jesus those burdens that are weighing us down.

Jesus knew that this was an exercise that would require many repetitions before it would ever become ingrained in our spirit's muscle memory. But it is possible. When we have truly begun to trust the Lord with ALL our hearts and to acknowledge Him in ALL our ways… forgiveness can become muscle memory. Just a natural reaction to offenses on this journey of faith.

Forgiveness

It's Supernatural!

Many people never attempt to engage in the process of forgiveness. They think that forgiveness is something that they must accomplish in their own strength. God gives grace to the humble (James 4:6,7) and His strength is perfect when your strength is gone. (2 Corinthians 12:9,10) God needs for you to decide to forgive—this gives Him permission to assist you in the process. Forgiveness is a choice!

We choose forgiveness by humbling ourselves before God to the obedience of His word. To do this we have to cast aside every malicious thought that satan brings to justify our anger. Matthew 11:25 KJV says, "And when ye stand praying, forgive, if ye have aught against any: that your Father also which is in heaven may forgive you your trespasses."

Acknowledge God amidst your frustration, anger, and pain. He already sees and knows, and—He gets it. The Bible tells us to pour out our complaints before Him. (Psalm 142:2) It also tells us that when we humble ourselves in the sight of the Lord, He will lift us. (James 4:10). Once we act in obedience, we have involved God in the equation. Just like salvation is an act of faith—so is forgiveness. God gives grace to the humble. The more we humble ourselves—the more grace He gives to begin and complete the journey and process of forgiveness.

Life has afforded me many opportunities to rely on the Holy Spirit to walk me through forgiving others. Several times, I felt the immediate impact of the power of forgiveness operating in my heart. On one occasion, a woman that my Pastor paired me with to work on a project was rude and condescending towards me and another member in front of others. She was so wrong!

I was incensed with anger! Anger gripped me to the point that I could not worship without scoping out the other side of the church where she was seated. "How can she sing and raise her hands like that! So hypocritical!" I thought.

"Ask her to forgive you." The Lord spoke. I argued, "*Why? I didn't* do nothing!" I have learned whenever I engage in a disagreement with God to always side with Him in the end. I did as He instructed. I approached her the next Sunday and said, "Forgive me for my response during our last conversation." Short and sweet. *IMMEDIATELY*...I felt something eject from my heart! What was satan trying to do to me! What kind of venomous fruit had he planted inside of me? Who would I be today if I had never accepted the antidote of forgiveness? I don't think it would be the person that I have transformed into today: someone who respects, acknowledges, and utilizes the power of forgiveness.

The Bible warns us to guard our hearts with *all* diligence (meaning be very, very careful) because the issues of life flow from it. (Proverbs 4:12) Understand this: satan impales your heart with fiery darts, and offense occurs. His goal is to duplicate in you the exact toxic behaviors of the person who inflicted you with a wound. He desires to replicate his character and produce corrupt fruit in your life— and others, so that you can spend eternity with Him—in hell!

Satan is amused when we surrender to hatred and unforgiveness resulting from his maneuvers. You become his trophy—his prize to illustrate that he was victorious in deceiving and destroying you. Walking in love and forgiveness is the only way to counteract the destructive aftermath of unforgiveness. As long as you walk in anger and hatred seeking your own vindication you are cooperating with the wrong spirit. God is our vindicator! (Isaiah 50:8)

16

The Bible tells us that our battle is **NOT** with flesh and blood (Read Ephesians the 6th Chapter)—people find this spiritual reality difficult to digest and insist on focusing their need for revenge on each other. Forgiveness acts as a supernatural potion with the power to neutralize the schemes and assignments that unforgiveness sets in motion in our lives.

In Jeremiah 1:10, God tells Jeremiah to use words to root out, tear down, plant, and build. This is exactly what forgiveness does. When forgiveness is utilized, mother and daughter are no longer feuding. Walls of anger and separation are torn down. Father is no longer against son. Brother is no longer against brother nor sister against sister. The antidote of forgiveness creates space in the heart for seeds of love, trust, and restoration to blossom.

Even during these perilous times, the power of forgiveness is destroying years of destruction that have resulted in unforgiveness. Forgiveness will set in motion a season of restoration. Just like forgiveness is a process—so is restoration. Some processes of forgiveness will result in reconciliation. This can be immediate, or a relationship is restored over time. Once you and another have agreed to forgive; you may be in for a bumpy ride—be patient with the recovery process.

Forgiveness

Keeping it *Real*

Whether you are new to the faith, never committed your heart to Jesus or been in the church 50 years. Jesus is Our Savior and the one which we owe our all. When will people stop turning their back on God "because the church is full of hypocrites? Because your pastor offended you? Because they didn't recognize your gift? Because she looked at me funny? Because nobody likes me? The list goes on and on. This list did not include many of the more hideous offenses that many have suffered from strangers, family, friends, or co-workers.

Yet whether big or small; when offenses remain unaddressed some people choose to no longer live a life surrendered to God. God is the One who so loved you that He sent His Son to lay down His life for **YOU**.

People will fail us—You must forgive... You will disappoint yourself—You must forgive... You may be angry at God—You must forgive... If you want to stand before God justified in the end...You **MUST** forgive!

Forgiveness

Is a Choice

While developing this book, I struggled with the book cover. I asked different ones for their input and came up with some interesting options. When I shared my cover images with a creative friend, she said, "Maybe you are trying to be too literal." I prayed and listened for direction and clarity. I cleaned up the original book cover drafts that I was considering. I heard the Lord say, "I need people to take the matter of forgiveness *literally*. I stuck with the original cover with a bottle with the words *"The Antidote."*

It really is that simple. Unforgiveness has poisoned and prevented many from moving fully into the plans and purposes of God. It has diminished the quality of life because of physical incapacitation. It has stripped countless of love, joy, and peace. God has provided an antidote—forgiveness. We are in a battle called life. No one escapes life without being impaled by satan's fiery darts. With every wound resulting in offense, we have a choice whether to allow these wounds to fester, spread, and cause complications—Or simply accept the remedy that God freely offers.

If we can only picture that when we are told that forgiveness is for you foremost— this is a reality—not a trick! I watched a documentary about an urban neighborhood. A number of families lost loved ones through gang violence. I was half asleep and managed to capture the end of the show. The families and community of supportive neighbors and friends were grieving. They banned together and convinced everyone to join a march.

Some of the families of the victims were reluctant, but, in the end, I think they all participated.

Their peaceful demonstration consisted of a notable-sized group funneling through the community chanting these words… **"I choose to forgive! I choose to forgive! I choose to forgive!"**

Their words penetrated the atmosphere in unison as they canvassed the neighborhood. They knew their agonizing cries would be heard by the murderers. Many had tears in their eyes as the words rolled from their lips. Yet they chose to partake of the antidote of forgiveness to allow the healing process to begin. This doesn't mean that their pain, anger, grief, bitterness, and other deep-seated emotions just vanished! Choosing forgiveness does not mean that these normal responses to pain will magically disappear. Forgiveness is not always a quick fix, but it opens the heart and activates the potent healing properties of forgiveness.

On the battlefield of life, many have lost loved ones to murder, and hideous abuses may have been done to you or others that you love. Forgiveness is the last thing you want to consider—especially if it is seen as something given to the ones responsible for your pain. Take a moment and visualize forgiveness as a healing potion that God offers—because He so loves you. Receive it! It will appease *YOUR* pain. Because it is so potent it has the power to impact others that are present and leaning towards unforgiveness once it is released. It is an antidote with the ability to arrest, heal, and prevent the rapid spread of the dreadful disease process of unforgiveness in your physical, emotional, and spiritual body.

Below are words that I practice releasing often into the atmosphere. Even small unforgiveness infections can spread into something that chokes the life from you over time if unaddressed. Repeat the I choose to forgive prayer in the next section or create your own. Add it to your forgiveness workout routine.

TODAY, I
CHOOSE to Forgive

God, I surrender my mind, will, and emotions.   All whom have hurt me, TODAY I CHOOSE TO FORGIVE…

All whom have spoken all manner of evil against me; TODAY I CHOOSE TO FORGIVE…

All whom have overlooked or rejected me; TODAY I CHOOSE TO FORGIVE…

All whom I have loved unconditionally, shown mercy, sown seed and given my heart only to have them to trample it; TODAY I CHOOSE TO FORGIVE…

All whom have lied to me, lied on me and used me for their own personal gain; TODAY I CHOOSE TO FORGIVE…

All who have traumatized me to the depths of my being creating spiritual, emotional, physical, sexual or any other diabolical insults to my being; TODAY I CHOOSE TO FORGIVE…

Those that are no longer in the land of the living and wounded my life in any manner; whether physical, emotional, sexual spiritual abuse or otherwise; TODAY I CHOOSE TO FORGIVE…

For the times that I have been repulsed, angry or unforgiving towards myself; TODAY I CHOOSE TO FORGIVE…

For the times that I was angry at You God; because my faith failed, I did not understand, and I failed to trust; TODAY I CHOOSE TO FORGIVE…

Forgiveness

Time to Open the Door

*G*od knew that while living in a fallen world that we would adopt behaviors that would result in anger, bitterness, and hatred—the fruit of unforgiveness. The scripture tells us that Jesus is standing and knocking our door and that if *anyone* opens, He will come in and sup with us (Revelation 3:20). Many relegate this scripture merely to receiving salvation, but this is for ANYTHING that we are in need of hashing out with the Lord. Just like the physical heart; the spiritual heart has chambers or rooms. We all have rooms that Jesus is yet seeking entrance. Often unforgiveness is buried deep inside the inner chambers of our hearts; tucked safely away from everyone, sometimes hidden even from ourselves.

When anyone attempts to enter these secluded chambers—access is denied. Imagine Jesus standing before you with His hands extended holding a potion with the ability to heal the pain and anger in your heart. All you have to do is receive it. That potion is His very own blood which was shed for the remission of our sins. When we allow Him to enter and we accept the healing balm of forgiveness; we discover that it is not our strength, but God's unlimited strength and power flowing through us. God empowers us to offer the antidote of forgiveness to others.

Just like satan seeks to replicate and spread the process of unforgiveness. Jesus wants to do the same with forgiveness.

Once we accept the antidote from Him; we can choose to offer it to others. It is your time to knock on the door of the hearts of others that you desire to give or receive forgiveness. God grants each of us generous portions of the antidote of forgiveness to freely

23

share with others. God is with you, don't hesitate, you can do it! Choose to forgive—*TODAY!*

Humility

the

Door to Forgiveness

---

*H*ow can you always have yourself under control when others hurt you; many times, intentionally? Others may hurt you daily; *especially* those in your own household! We need strategies!

Gather the essential tools in this book to not only help you to walk, move and elevate like a winner but dominate like one too! We *CAN* defeat satan in the area of unforgiveness. God gave us the upper hand, but we only need to find the faith and courage to use it. The weapons of our warfare are not physical; but when we learn to trust and utilize them in our spiritual battles, we will witness their great power. Let's face it; we will forever face challenges loaded with opportunities to both give and receive forgiveness. Arming yourself with a conscious *decision* to walk in forgiveness *before* your feet hit the floor in the morning prepares you for effective battle.

The Bible tells us that in the last days, father would be against son and mother against daughter and that our foes would be those in our own households. (Matthew 10:35,36). Satan is no fool; at least not when it comes to destroying lives. He knows the best way to throw any of us off our game, is to create chaos and unforgiveness with those that we hold nearest and dearest. The book of Ephesians instructs us to put on the whole armor of God. I think the people of God do, but we tend to toss it aside when amongst family and friends. This is not Biblical. Newsflash! There is **NO** safety zone!

Nowhere in the bible does it say that we are to take our armor off. satan is constantly seeking our destruction and waits for vulnerable moments to pounce. Think about it...where are the origins of some of your deepest emotional wounds? Most likely family and friends! Some families have learned to do effective spiritual warfare in these areas and walk in a practice of forgiveness that is necessary to enjoy lives enriched with love, forgiveness, and peace. Yet many family relationships have been strategically dismantled by the wiles and deception of the devil. Nothing brings satan greater joy. He has impacted future generations by rupturing vital relationships. Grandchildren, nieces, nephews are left without the voice of the elder relations to impart wisdom and direction. With this protective layer of counselors removed they become easy prey for the enemy.

If this is your story; this does *not* have to be how it ends. God is a Restorer and He can mend *anything* that satan has ripped apart. When God rebuilds, He can fortify and make it even stronger than before. Someone has to have the courage to act in humility to begin the process. In Jeremiah 1:10 God set Jeremiah over the House of Israel "to root out, and to pull down, and to destroy, and to throw down, to build, and to plant." This is exactly what has to occur for the healing process to be completed in our hearts. This is all done by the strategic use of words, words spoken by the wisdom, love, and direction of the Holy Spirit.

When I sought definitions for humility; the act of being humble was often used. But what is being humble? My definition is "**power under restraint**." It works for me. Imagine humility being a door. A door that you can walk through with one goal in mind...forgiveness. *Not* to prove who was wrong or right. *Not* to say, "I told you so." *Not* to seek vengeance or vindication...merely cleaning the slate and entering to give—or receive a good old fashion dose of forgiveness.

Wait! You might think you are ready, but before you reach for that doorknob; there are some things you need to keep in mind. I am certain there is more, but I will list three.

1. Speak the truth in love.
(Ephesians 4:15)

Too often the truth is smashed into our faces without mercy, love or compassion and with the *wrong* motives. People often feel that this is okay and as long as they are telling the *truth*—they are covered. But *ple—aase* read to the end of the scripture. Serving the *truth* sandwiched in *love* is a sign of spiritual maturity. It is the love component of the truth that pierces the stony hearts, rips away the dark veil from the mind preventing the light and causes the hearer to be receptive.

Love is a healing balm to a wounded spirit and increases the potential for a positive outcome. Will everyone readily accept what you said once you have done this? They may gladly receive what you are saying, or maybe they will later—or perhaps never! You cannot control how others respond when you give or ask for forgiveness; even when you speak-the-truth-in-love. Yet you can walk away feeling assured that you have done what God requires of you. The seeds of your words are planted, and God can cause the fruit of forgiveness to be produced in their hearts over time.

2. Be more ready to listen than to speak when you go to God's house. (Ecclesiastes 5:1)

Where is God's house? It is you and I; for our bodies are the temples of the living God. Life has taught me that things are rarely as they seem. When you enter through the door of humility and engage in the process of heart to heart sharing you may discover that either yours, the other persons—or both perceptions were totally off! Misconceptions by one or both parties may have caused a prolonged breakdown in the relationship.

27

Damages can extend into years and sometimes are never repaired at all because of a misperception. Too many times, we walk away angry when what was **said** and what was **heard** does not reflect what was **meant.** Your head may be racing with words that you desire to express. Give ample time to allow the other person to speak—pay attention rather than mentally rehearsing your response! A decision to listen with an open mind and receptive heart can accelerate the process of restoration. Such sacred moments cause satan to cringe. Let's make him cringe!

3. Death and life are in the power of the tongue. (Proverbs 18:22)

Say it! I'm sorry or forgive me; either is just two words—they are powered packed. How many times has reconciliation failed though nice, elaborate and soothing words may have been spoken? But... I'm sorry, forgive me or—I forgive you...were *not* included. The wounded person leaves feeling slighted; carrying a *partial* or maybe even a full grudge. This grudge may be potent enough to continue to produce roots of bitterness, anger, strife and more unforgiveness. Is it worth it? Why expend emotional energy for something that becomes nothing more than a fruitless gesture and a confirmation of your pride? Just say the words!

"FORGIVE ME! I'M SORRY!" "I FORGIVE YOU!"

The world will not end because you humbled yourself.
Your hand is on the knob of the door. You are preparing to enter. Take a moment to practice a few times before you turn that knob! Satan will surely try to choke you before you get them out.

Repeat it... *"Forgive me."* Or *"I'm sorry."*

28

These words don't make you a wimp; they are actually a manifestation of your strength, humility, and obedience to the Word of God. This is an outward manifestation of the power of the Holy Spirit abiding and operating through you. It is worth it just to experience a sense that your Father, God is well-pleased with you.

The Other
Side of the Door

Before deciding upon the best strategy make sure that you have regained your composure; if it is a situation that does not require immediate remediation. If you find that you are angry and emotionally charged; spend some time putting things into a clear perspective. Consult with God on what's the best approach. Be prayerful and once you feel ready; check to see that you have on the full armor of God. Take a deep breath, turn the knob and enter through the door of humility with these strategies in mind.

1. Begin with "I" statements. When possible, avoid using "YOU" statements.

This is one of many effective communication strategies. When the *FIRST* word a person hears is *"YOU"* they may immediately turn on defenses and not hear anything else in your message. It may leave them feeling targeted or blamed for something that they feel none or only partial responsibility for. If already angry this can pour even more fuel on their anger decreasing the possibilities for a positive outcome.

Using I statement such as; "I felt hurt when I heard those words…" Rather than… "You hurt me… You always… You never…" Using I statements may help the other person to see that you are focusing on your perception of the situation and not trying to interpret their motives, feelings or intents. This can be a bridge to hear each other and communicate what you really wanted the other party to hear and understand.

31

2.   Lower your voice.

Whether approaching someone to give or receive forgiveness… the conversation may become heated and voice levels may surge. If the person that you are talking to gets louder… continue to lower your voice. This will make it necessary for them to lower their voice in order to hear you. If this is not effective it may be necessary to explain that you would really like to come to a place of peace and will approach the issue when you both are able to address concerns in a reasonable manner.

3.   Identify the conditions of the proposed interaction.

This is my favorite. For example, "I want to have a conversation with you. I need you to allow me to finish speaking before you respond. Then I will allow you to complete your thoughts before I speak. Are you willing to do this? If there is an agreement move forward. You may further suggest that if they need to take a moment to gather their thoughts that this will be okay. Many times, others will agree to this if they are wanting to reconcile or put the issues behind them. If they are not; you can still ask for or give forgiveness before ending the conversation. You can walk away knowing that you have done what God requires and continue to pray for total restoration if that is what you are seeking.

4.   Write a letter.

This technique will not work for everyone as not all are effective with written communication. Some people have difficulty expressing themselves verbally and can do better with writing. When addressing concerns verbally; the discussion could become heated resulting in more anger. A letter gives you an opportunity to fully express yourself before emotional tensions rise.

When writing (use I statements) and request that they reply in writing if they are comfortable with doing this. If not, allow time for their verbal response. Depending on the sensitivity of the issue, you may want to avoid referring to written concerns in detail. Be discreet. Use vague terms like; "the issue that has come between us…" or "The situation that occurred yesterday…"

 ### 5.   Say the words. FORGIVE ME…

I know that this was already mentioned, but it is *REALLY* important and worthy of repetition. That was the whole point of going through the door in the first place. Don't give an elaborate speech and omit saying the healing words that are infused with power and petrifies the enemy. ***Forgive me, I'm sorry… or I forgive you.*** Satan knows that these words have the power and potential to rebuild everything that he has strategically destroyed in that relationship.

Let's clean the slate of our lives with God— and man.
1. Make a list of people you may need to forgive.

_____
_____
_____
_____

2. Make a list of people that have offended you.

_____
_____
_____
_____

3. Ask the Holy Spirit to give you a specific approach for each person. Review the strategies in this book and choose one. God knows how each one of us is wired and what will be the most effective method.

"For if you forgive men their trespasses, your heavenly Father will also forgive you: But if you forgive not men their trespasses, neither will your Father forgive your trespasses. (Matthew 6:14.15) This alone is enough motivation and reason to turn that knob and go through the door of humility. Forgiveness is a spiritual weapon; use it!

Forgiveness

The Legacy

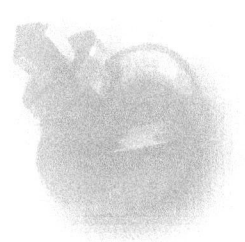

" Forgive me." As a mother, I have spoken these words to my children many times over the years. When we as parents invest in such practices, in many cases, it is a gift to them. While working in mental health for years I have seen parents who expressed no remorse when their children grow up and express anger. In their eyes, they gave their child *EVERYTHING...*

At least from their perspective. As knowledge about emotional needs increases, we are expanding in the area of effective use of "love languages." We are learning that we all have specific actions that communicate love to us. Sometimes as parents (using parents but can apply to any relationship), we may give *EVERYTHING, EXCEPT* the *ONE THING* that best communicates love to your child.

No matter how great a parent you are; it is quite possible that your child may have harbored some unexpressed frustration or bitterness that was buried over the years. Because their love may have covered a multitude of faults (just as a parent's love covers faults) they may have felt no need to profess them to you. Then there is the matter of satan's destructive efforts that results in widespread addictions of all sort and perverted behaviors for many young adult parents with children.

Negative behaviors created by addictions may stop once you surrender your heart to God; but the emotional impact on others; *especially* your children will likely continue to bear fruit of unforgiveness. God can cause restoration in these relationships—though it can be quite the emotional journey.

We are creating a legacy with the manner that we handle anger and conflict.

Sometimes two families are angry at each other for generations. (Not necessarily relatives.) Perhaps you saw a movie with the story of the *Hatfield's and the McCoy's?* There have been many movie remakes through the years of this true event. The date the feuding started is obscure, but around the time of the Civil War. One family was Confederate, and the other Unionist. This was thought to be the cause of the division. We certainly see great animosity created by opposing political views today!

Their hatred may have been fortified by someone stealing a hog. Though the facts are uncertain the aftermath is well documented. Each family had at least 13 children who hated each other because the parents hated each other. It started with an occasional physical brawl and escalated to murdering each other and burning down homes. It's documented that this feud ended in 1891, some descendants shook hands in 1976 and actually signed a peace treaty in 2003. Are you connected to gangs that carry grudges that result in the senseless deaths of innocent people? Are you allowing your anger, hatred or unforgiveness towards a particular family, race, group or political party to filter into the next generation?

Children watch and learn who to hate from parental figures. We are creating legacies. This legacy can determine how forgiveness is perceived, received and given throughout future generations. Will your legacy be one that exemplifies humbling yourself to the obedience of the Word of God? Will the message and example that you extend to future generations be one of love? Or hatred? Forgiveness? Or Unforgiveness? Regardless of what was done by your forefathers—the ball's in your court now…

Forgiveness

Cinderella

T Here are so many versions of the epic fairy tale titled, "Cinderella." I have read many books and watched numerous versions of this film over the years. Yet my favorite is a movie I watched a couple of years ago. Its ending left such an emotional impact and a great visual demo of forgiveness. The evil stepmother confessed her hatred to Cinderella and the reasons why she was despised. With a heart putrid with jealousy, she glared at her and screamed, "You are young, beautiful and kind..." This was not meant to be a compliment. These words described everything that the evil stepmother was not, and they were laced with virulent poisons of bitterness, envy, and hatred. Cinderella was reviled and treated cruel for no reason. The more her light shone the greater her afflictions. Our story as Christians can have highlights depicted by fiery trials arising merely because we are beautiful and kind. Salvation beautifies.

Jesus made it no secret that when following Him that we *would* suffer persecution. He reassured us that this is no cause to worry because He has overcome the world and is committed to helping each of us to do the same. (John 16:33) God's grace is sufficient to help us to emerge as victors against the vicious satanic onslaughts that each of us will face at some point in our lives. Yet we must be mindful to follow biblical instructions.

When satan assigns someone to break you; like in the fictional account of Cinderella; His goal is to reproduce within you that same corrupt character. Then you become accessible for his use to unleash your pent-up anger and frustrations on others. This cycle of reproducing hearts infected with unforgiveness spreading from person to person repeats until we have an epidemic of hostile masses who all *"feel some type of way!"* Some of them get guns and execute innocent people in public places. Many vile acts of hatred are committed from these poisoned hearts. We must learn to protect our hearts and to self-administer the antidote of forgiveness as often as needed; the supply is limitless.

In the make-believe story of Cinderella, the abused and neglected servant girl did exactly as the bible instructs everyone to do. "Guard your heart with all diligence, for out of it flows the issues of life." (Proverbs 4:23) Walking out of the home of her evil stepmother, the Prince held her hand while walking close by her side. Before reaching the door, she paused just long enough to connect with the furious eyes of her evil stepmother. "I forgive you," her gentle voice released these words, and the atmosphere was perfumed with their kindness and sincerity. She walked out the door leaving behind a place filled with memories of slavery, rejection, and humiliation. Holding onto her Prince she stepped into the bright future awaiting.

Abuse may cause your heart to become a storehouse where unforgiveness is hoarded. Satan will tell you that you have good reasons to hold onto every bitter emotion while dragging your life downhill. No one would argue that many people have undisputable *reasons* to choose unforgiveness. I had some pretty good ones myself. But none of us have the *right.*

Cinderella is just a fictional character, and we can make light of her selfless act of forgiveness. After all, it was just a fairy tale with an ending orchestrated by the strokes of an author's pen. But Jesus' selfless act of forgiveness was done on a universal scale and it was orchestrated not by the ink of a written story; but by the blood streaming from His wounded body.

While hanging from a cross, beaten, bleeding, and dying. He thought more about this suffering world than Himself. He held back death long enough to grant forgiveness to a thief hanging and dying beside Him. Before taking His final breath, He looked into the faces of the angry mob that mocked Him and upon those who brutally beat Him until the skin ripped from His flesh and then nailed Him onto the cross. "Father, forgive them, for they know not what they do." The atmosphere was perfumed by the abundant love that He felt for all humanity. Letting go of this life, He eagerly anticipated returning to heavenly places to take His seat at the right hand of His Father.

This is the most powerful illustration of forgiveness that this world will ever know. Jesus is your Prince of Peace. Just like in the story of Cinderella, you can grasp the hand of your Prince, and He will escort you out of the darkness where unforgiveness has kept you imprisoned. Walk with Him and trust Him; he is leading you into a brighter place.

Forgiveness

What About You?

To thine own self be true. Selfish? I used to think so until I read the next line written by Shakespeare. "...thou canst not then be false to any man." It is difficult to convince another that God so loves them if you are struggling with believing that He so loves you. There are many drowning in the murky waters of unforgiveness—for themselves.

Satan has mastered the skill of hammering people with lies and accusations. Remorseful memories of the past can parade through your head—on repeat mode. Many people struggle with feeling disconnected, unloved and unworthy. When they do manage to muster enough faith to believe that God has forgiven them; they are not able to squeeze enough faith to extend forgiveness to themselves. I know the sadness this produces as I have certainly been there.

Can you imagine what this must look like from Jesus's perspective? You approach the throne of God time and time again repenting for the same thing over and over. Why? Because you are carrying a weight that Jesus has agreed to carry for you. Because you don't feel deserving; you will not release it to Him. Do you realize what you have done?

You have aligned your agreement with the lies of satan instead of the word of God. There is a reason that God instructs us to cast down *every* thought that exalts itself above the knowledge of God (2 Corinthians 10:5). Jesus stands waiting and willing to remove the burden of your sin, but you hold onto them tightly. He remembers the price He paid for your freedom and tries to reassure you that He loves you and is willing and able to help. His life—such a great ransom offered for you—because you are a prized possession. He died for your sins and the sins of the world. You believe that the sins of the world are forgiven...but you just cannot incorporate this forgiveness for yourself.

It is like telling Him; Thank you for dying for the sins of the world, and though your Blood has been effective for many—it just hasn't worked for me." Do you realize what a slap in the face this must feel like for Him! Yet He stands, He knocks... Let Him in. He will relieve the burden of unforgiveness for yourself today. There is therefore *NOW* NO CONDEMNATION to them that are in Christ Jesus (Romans 8:1).

Pray for the Holy Spirit to assist you with the process of counting yourself worthy of YOUR love, of GOD'S love. You are worthy of YOUR forgiveness and GOD'S forgiveness. You do not have to beat yourself for your sin—Jesus has already taken your beating. Just let it go and follow Him...

Arm Yourself Likewise

Often people come to Jesus
Because they need relief
The problems of this world
Has caused them suffering and grief.

Accepting Christ into their hearts
Festered wounds began to heal
The brokenness of their soul
He restores and rebuilds.

Wouldn't it be nice
To right here end this chapter
With those famous last words
"They lived happily ever after."

You were thinking "My pain is over"
My suffering is through!
And begin to feel betrayed
When new trials came to you.

Let's take a moment to reflect
On the life of Jesus Christ
He was pure, He was holy
And He always walked upright.

He suffered greatly in this world
And quite unjustly so
I wonder how He felt inside?
You and I may never know.
He chose to love His persecutors

Though betrayed and falsely accused
Then for their iniquities
He was wounded, beaten and bruised.

Though legions of angels He commanded
He chose to suffer and die
Having a Heavenly Father
Willing to heed His faintest cry.

You want to be just like Him?
Are you willing to pay the price?
Abundant blessings await you
But there are some sacrifices.

One thing to remember
When facing worry and despair
Shut off the voice of satan
Don't let Him whisper in your ear.

He will say you're all alone
God has forsaken you and left
And you might as well give up
Rather than taking another step.

He will tell you that God's the reason
For everything you're going through
Of all the things He tells you
None of them will be the truth.

The time is now to arm yourself
Put on the very mind of Christ
Let God get all the glory.
For the suffering in your life.

He's not the cause of your suffering
He's the cure for your pain.
While satan's plan and purpose
Is to drive you insane!

Forgiveness

The Process

Acknowledge

Ever seen someone seething with anger while spouting out the words, "I'm *not* mad!" You have to acknowledge that there is a concern that needs addressing and decide to choose the pathway of forgiveness.

Surrender

Salvation starts with a heart that is surrendered to God acknowledging that you need Him to successfully face the challenges of this life. You are not able to truly love unconditionally until the love of God is shed abroad in your heart (Romans 5:5).

So, it is with forgiveness. You are not able to bear the burden of unforgiveness. As you allow the Holy Spirit to participate in the process by shedding the Spirit of forgiveness in our hearts; you begin to realize and understand that by God's grace, forgiveness is doable.

Unlearning

All of us have been taught myths and given erroneous information about forgiveness and what it is and is not. Misinformation may have resulted in deciding that it is impossible for you to forgive certain situations. Disregard the myths and act upon strategies that will equip and prepare you to tread the path of forgiveness with truth and courage. You are so much stronger than you think you are, and when you are weak; the God in you is yet strong.

45

Approach

A particular approach may work better in some situations than others. Prayerfully consider each situation and the person or persons involved and ask the Holy Spirit to direct you to the plan that will work best.

Look over the strategies provided in this book or those given to you by others that speak into your life. The Holy Spirit will lead you in the way that you should go. Trust Him.

Patience

Just like healing occurs at different rates for those that have undergone illness or surgical procedures; it is the same when recovering from unforgiveness. Unforgiveness creates actual wounds in our spirits. There are cuts, bruises and even infections in our spiritual beings. Some physical healings are miraculous, others occur in stages over a period of time. The power of forgiveness can result in a supernatural occurrence of immediate healing. Then for some it is a process where the pain dissipates over time with a restoration of peace of mind. It is a process that demands faith and patience.

Do not align yourself with the lies of satan. "See you haven't forgiven…because if you had you wouldn't feel…" Or other similar deceits. We do not walk by feelings, but by faith.

satan tries to bring condemnation to you about your salvation even when you have been giving your all to God. He pinpoints your shortcomings and attempts to deceive you. He desires to rob you of your testimony of salvation. If you agree with him, he will rob you of your commitment to forgive. When he comes with lies (and he will) tell him, I CHOOSE TO FORGIVE. Align your faith with the word of God and pray for the person that you have forgiven. "Resist the devil and he will flee" (James 4:7).

Parable

of the

Unforgiving Servant

Then Peter came to Him and said, "Lord, how often shall my brother sin against me, and I forgive him? Up to seven times?"

Jesus said to him, "I do not say to you, up to seven times, but up to seventy times seven. Therefore, the kingdom of heaven is like a certain king who wanted to settle accounts with his servants. And when he had begun to settle accounts, one was brought to him who owed him ten thousand talents. But as he was not able to pay, his master commanded that he be sold, with his wife and children and all that he had, and that payment be made. The servant therefore fell down before him, saying, 'Master, have patience with me, and I will pay you all.' Then the master of that servant was moved with compassion, released him, and forgave him the debt.

"But that servant went out and found one of his fellow servants who owed him a hundred denarii; and he laid hands on him and took *him* by the throat, saying, 'Pay me what you owe!' So his fellow servant fell down at his feet and begged him, saying, 'Have patience with me, and I will pay you all. And he would not but went and threw him into prison till he should pay the debt. So, when his fellow servants saw what had been done, they were very grieved, and came and told their master all that had been done. Then his master, after he had called him, said to him, 'You wicked servant! I forgave you all that debt because you begged me. Should you not also have had compassion on your fellow servant, just as I had pity on you?' And his master was angry and delivered him to the torturers until he should pay all that was due to him.

"So My heavenly Father also will do to you if each of you, from his heart, does not forgive his brother his trespasses."

Matthew 18:21–35

Forgiveness

Myths

Many myths have attached themselves to
teachings on forgiveness. Much of it is done
because it is what we have heard taught over the years. There is
great freedom in knowing and operating in truth. Though there
are many more; I have identified some myths below. Perhaps some
the myths listed below have caused you to question if you are really
walking in forgiveness. Or maybe you ran across some and decided
that if this is true; forgiveness is not the path for you.

I pray that this book has caused you to reconsider any erroneous
beliefs that you had about forgiveness. I pray that you will
experience the potent power and freedom that forgiveness offers.
It is God's remedy for the hearts of His people that have been
mutilated in the battles of this life during our struggle to live
together in this fallen world.

Reflect upon the myths listed below and identify whether they
have influenced your ability to understand and commit to the
process of forgiveness.

MYTH: If you forgive someone, you should forget it
ever happened.

TRUTH: Forgiveness and forgetting are two very different
things.

MYTH: Forgiveness is a decision an act of the will.

TRUTH: Forgiveness is a decision *and* a process.

MYTH: Forgiveness and reconciliation are the same things.

TRUTH: Forgiveness and reconciliation are very different things.

MYTH: After I forgive, I will never feel angry or hurt about it again:

TRUTH: That's like saying after I get saved; I will never make a mistake or sin again. Or after I have surgery, I will not feel pain again. If angry feelings resurface and more than likely they will—continue to release them back to the Lord and allow deeper healing to occur.

MYTH: Forgiveness means you are the weaker person

TRUTH: Anyone can operate in pride and stubbornness; it takes humility and the strength of God to forgive.

MYTH: Forgiveness means you have to trust them.

TRUTH: You may never be able to trust someone you have forgiven again—in fact in some cases it is wise not to.

Prayer

Forgiving Others

God, I hurt, I am angry, I don't understand why I was treated this way. I don't feel like I deserved it. The pain in my heart is overwhelming and it consumes me. I need your help. The kind of help that can only come from you. Forgive me for the anger and resentment that I have allowed to fester in my heart. It is beginning to impact every area of my life. I do not wish to continue this way. Forgiving would be much easier if they showed some remorse. Nevertheless, I choose to forgive _____. I know that I cannot change how _____ reacts towards me, but help me to respond in a way that pleases you. Holy Spirit I ask for your Spirit of Wisdom, Knowledge, and Understanding when it is necessary to communicate with _____. I trust in You Lord with all my heart and I cast this care upon You.

In Jesus name,

Amen

Prayer

Self-Forgiveness

God, I don't know why you love me; but I am grateful. I know that the Bible says that you love me and when I asked, You forgave me of **ALL** my sins. Yet I find it hard to love and forgive myself. Forgive me for listening and agreeing with the voice of the enemy and acting as if what he says is true. The things that I have committed in my past keep replaying in my head and I can't stop them. When they come, I feel unclean and unworthy to stand in your presence. Cleanse me through and through.

Cleanse my mind, Cleanse my heart. Cleanse my emotions. Holy Spirit help me to think thoughts that are pure, lovely and true. Forgive me for acting as the blood of your Son, Jesus was insufficient to help me with self-forgiveness. Today, I stand in agreement with your word that there is *now* **NO** condemnation to those who are in Christ. Today, I resist the devil and he flees! Today, I put on the whole armor of God. Holy Spirit remind me of this commitment that I have made before my Father God this day and help me to cast down every deceiving thought and quiet every lying voice.

Today I align my heart, mind, will, and emotions with what Your word says about me. God, I accept your forgiveness and today I forgive myself. I cast down every diabolical thought that challenges my spiritual identity as your Beloved Son/Daughter. I am made worthy by your Blood and again I say, Thank You.

In Jesus Name,
Amen

Forgiveness Scriptures

Forbearing one another, and forgiving one
another, if any man has a quarrel against any: even as Christ
forgave you, so also do ye.
Colossians 3:13 KJV

For if ye forgive men their trespasses, your heavenly Father will
also forgive you: But if ye forgive not men their trespasses,
neither will your Father forgive your trespasses.
Matthew 6:14. 15 KJV

Take heed to yourselves: If thy brother trespass against thee,
rebuke him; and if he repent, forgive him.
Luke 17:3 KJV

In whom we have redemption through his blood, the forgiveness
of sins, according to the riches of his grace,
Ephesians 1:7 KJV

And forgive us our debts, as we forgive our debtors.
Matthew 6:12 KJV

For this is my blood of the new testament,
which is shed for many for the remission of sins.
Matthew 26:28 KJV

Epilogue

What does the sacrament of communion mean to you? I thought I was finished with this book, but I clearly sensed the Lord urging me to address this practice which is common to most churches. *"Do this in remembrance of me,"* was Jesus's instructions before His death, resurrection, and ascension. I engage in communion in my home with the Lord often. I **NEVER** want to forget the cost of my freedom. What do you call to your remembrance before communion?

I allow my imagination to place me before the cross where there is just me and Jesus. I try, but I cannot imagine what my life would have been had he not rescued me. Would I be insane? Would I be in prison? Would I be on drugs? Would I be dead? Any one of these could have easily been my reality *without* His forgiveness.

I receive His love and forgiveness in my heart all over again as I examine myself. I search the depths of my heart to unveil any hidden chambers where unforgiveness may be breeding. Sometimes it is buried so deeply that you may not even realize that it is yet stashed. But as I stand at the cross overcome with gratitude and His love I choose to forgive. There is nothing in my heart that I refuse to release.

It is a good practice to live a life where we make giving and receiving forgiveness a norm. Especially with the minor irritations and grudges, we experience in our day to day lives. God knows and understands that some offences cut to the core of our beings; but the blood of Jesus is powerful enough to heal even our most incapacitating of our wounds, regardless of their nature. God understands that this is a process and warns us not to partake of communion until you have allowed the Holy Spirit to complete this process within you. The bible gives a stern warning against this practice that is ignored by many. Read I Corinthians 11:27-32; it illustrates how serious receiving communion is to God.

> **27**Wherefore whosoever shall eat this bread, and drink *this* cup of the Lord, unworthily, shall be

guilty of the body and blood of the Lord. But let a man examine himself, and so let him eat of *that* bread, and drink of *that* cup. **29**For he that eateth and drinketh unworthily, eateth and drinketh damnation to himself, not discerning the Lord's body. **30**For this cause many *are* weak and sickly among you, and many sleep. **31**For if we would judge ourselves, we should not be judged. **32**But when we are judged, we are chastened of the Lord, that we should not be condemned with the world.

In conclusion, it is extremely important that receiving communion not be seen as merely a ritual or tradition of the church. It is a time to remember that Jesus's blood was shed for the forgiveness of your sins. When you partake of communion as one who is *forgiven*—but unwilling to *forgive*—God considers you **UNWORTHY** to receive. Decide to allow the antidote of forgiveness to start a miraculous work in your heart **BEFORE** engaging in the sacrament of communion. When we choose to become a disciple of Jesus, the ***forgiven*** becomes the ***forgiver.***

NOTES

Author's Note

Whether ministering to others as speakers or writers, partner with the Holy Spirit. If we allow Him, He will maneuver us through the forgiveness process. Engaging in this process brings healing and restores peace. This allows us to arise and share our stories whether verbal or written from a position of power rather than pain.

Unforgiveness has the potential to stifle every area of our lives. To much of our lives are spent mentally rehearsing the emotional, spiritual or physical wounds inflicted upon us by others. When reliving these brutish episodes, the trauma can seem as fresh as if it happened yesterday.

Engaging the process of forgiveness helps you to disconnect from the pain over time. I am a writing coach and cross paths with those who feel called to write their stories but feel stuck. Some voice that writing causes them to relive devastating experiences that they long to forgive.

My prayer is my book has shed insight on how to take steps to freedom from the poison of unforgiveness. Are you one that God is calling to write? (We are all call to be His witness in some manner).

About the Author

Jeri Darby is an author, speaker, songwriter and writing coach. Her life journey has required huge doses of the forgiveness antidote. Jeri's earliest childhood memories are faded images of physical abuse. An older brother launched brutal physical assaults that continued into her adolescent years. This resulted in her entertaining murderous thoughts before receiving salvation.

Jeri has also been a victim of multiple rapes, kidnappings and emotional abuse over the years. She has learned to rely on God's strength in order to forgive herself and others. Her relationship with God has been her saving grace.

Overpowered by His love and acceptance she engaged in the process of forgiveness with the Holy Spirit. Jeri was able to express genuine love and forgiveness to her brother and lead him in a repenting prayer before his death.

Jeri served over twenty-five years in the mental health profession as a registered nurse. During this time, she developed deep compassion and empathy for others who have suffered abuses and experience the negative impact of unforgiveness. Jeri currently works with seniors. As she progresses further into her seasoned years she can identify with the challenges and concerns in this population.

God issued her a mandate in 2015 to create a Facebook Vlog aimed towards encouraging His seasoned people reminding them of the great love He has for them. Jeri has produced over 100 videos on this topic over the past two years. Replays can be viewed on Facebook: *Jeri Darby*. She is embracing her writing ministry during this season. This is the sixth book that she has authored and self-published while helping others to achieve their publishing dreams. Jeri finds joy in helping others to release their testimonies regarding the Faithfulness of God.

Her anointing as a writing coach has empowered others to dig deeper and to write with excellence at their highest level. Jeri has ministered in jails, prison, homeless shelters and spoken at conferences. She presided over Aglow International-Saginaw Lighthouse for over twelve years.

Despite every satanic onslaught, God caused her to arise even more fortified. One belief that is firmly rooted in Jeri's heart is that everything in her life has been a steppingstone and she uses the steppingstones of her life to soar into her destiny while helping others along the way.

OTHER TITLES BY JERI DARBY

TWO AVAILABLE IN SPANISH!

The Antidote

THIS BOOK UNVEILS ERRONEOUS BELIEFS ABOUT UNFORGIVENESS AND OFFERS BIBLICAL STRATEGIES FOR RESOLVING ISSUES OF UNFORGIVENESS.

GREAT RESOURCE FOR A FAMILY, SMALL GROUP OR CHURCH BIBLE STUDY.

CONTACT JERI AT 989 402-4721

IF YOU WOULD LIKE TO

HOST A FORGIVENESS BOOTCAMP

(LIVE OR ZOOM)

CONFERENCE OR OTHER EVENT,

1 DAY, WEEKEND OR SIX WEEKLY SESSIONS.

Say So!

★★★New Release★★★

Watch for Soon to be Released!

Contact Info

NEED A WRITING COACH?
SCHEDULE YOUR 20-MINUTE CONSULT

PHONE: 989 402-4721
EMAIL: JERI@IAMAWRITERNOW.COM

JOIN MY WRITER'S FB PAGE:
I AM A WRITER NOW

JOIN MY EMAIL LIST FOR FREE OFFERS AND UPDATES

Email List Nowsite

Visit my online Bookstore:

Online Bookstore